# The Spirit Power
# ~Volume II~

Grace Dola Balogun

"The fruit of the Spirit is

LOVE

JOY

PEACE

LONGSUFFERING

GENTLENESS

GOODNESS

FAITH

MEEKNESS

TEMPERANCE

Against such there is no law."

Galatians 5:22-23

# The Spirit Power
# ~Volume II~

Grace Dola Balogun

Grace Religious Books
New York, NY

The Spirit Power — Volume II
By Grace Dola Balogun
Copyright © 2012 Grace Dola Balogun
Cover design by Lionsgate Book Design, Lisa Hainline
www.lionsgatebookdesign.com
Interior Design by White Cottage Publishing Company
www.whitecottagepublishing.com

All rights reserved. No part of this book may be used or reproduced by any means, graphic, electronic, or mechanical, including photocopying, recording, taping, or by any information storage retrieval system without the written permission of the publisher except in the case of brief quotations embodied in critical articles and reviews.

Scripture quotations are from the King James Version of the Holy Bible.

Grace Religious Books Publishing & Distributors books may be ordered through booksellers or by contacting the publisher:

Grace Religious Books Publishing & Distributors, Inc.
213 Bennett Avenue
New York, NY 10040
www.Gracereligiousbookspublishers.com

To contact the author: 1-646-559-2533
info@gracereligiousbookspublishers.com

ISBN: 978-0-9851980-0-8 (epub)
SBN: 978-0-9851980-1-5 (pdf)
ISBN: 978-0-9851460-9-2 (sc)

Library of Congress Control Number: 20129334988

Printed in the United States of America

*I dedicate this book to the glory of my Lord and Savior Jesus Christ who emptied Himself, came to this earth to save me, a sinner, and blessed me with the salvation of eternal life in Him. May He receive glory, honor, blessings, and power from this book. May He let this book fill the hearts of everyone who reads it with the Spirit Power, now and forever. May Christ indwell, baptize, and fill the hearts of all who read this book with His Spirit. "But ye are not in the flesh, but in the Spirit, if so be that the Spirit of God dwell in you. Now if any man has not the Spirit of Christ, he is none of his." Rom 8:9. This book is from Him to make the power of the Holy Spirit manifest in the lives of all the children of God called by His name: Christians.*

# Contents

| | |
|---|---|
| Preface | vii |
| 1. Faithfulness | 1 |
| 2. Gentleness | 11 |
| 3. Self-Control | 16 |
| 4. Longsuffering | 27 |
| 5. Obedience | 31 |
| 6. Perseverance | 38 |
| 7. Forgiveness | 45 |
| 8. Forbearance | 50 |
| 9. Truth | 54 |
| 10. Temperance | 59 |
| 11. Humbleness | 64 |
| 12. Self-Esteem | 70 |
| 13. Righteousness | 77 |
| 14. Meekness | 85 |
| Summary | 93 |
| Bibliography | 98 |
| Biblical Index | 100 |
| Benediction | 105 |
| Other Books by the Author | 106 |
| About the Author | 110 |

# Preface

This Book, *The Spirit Power*, will let you know the power of the Spirit of God as you have never known it before: From the beginning of creation. It will clear away any confusion about the mighty power of the Holy Spirit, the saving Power of the Holy Spirit, and the Power of the fruit of the Holy Spirit that changes the believer's life.

This book will let you know that you need to be filled with the Holy Spirit; you need to be baptized with the Holy Spirit. This book will let you know the power of the indwelling of the Holy Spirit in the lives of believers immediately after conversion.

There is a difference between the indwelling of the Holy Spirit and the baptism of the Holy Spirit. The activities of the Holy Spirit on earth began on the day of the creation of the universe and have continued until the present.

The Holy Spirit is a living being, one of the three members of Godhead. He was active in creation and in sustaining the universe. He conceived Jesus in Mary's womb. He revealed God's will to men and gave the message of salvation. The Spirit also empowered the believers to perform miracles in order to confirm that their message was from God.

The Spirit dwells in the people of God today from the moment of conversion. When they are baptized by immersion, they claim open identification with Christ. If the Spirit of God does not indwell us, we are not a child of God. The Spirit will continue His work until the end of the world.

The Spirit's presence is the fullness of God's presence on earth in the lives of His people, the children of God. The Apostles received Holy Spirit baptism and they were speaking in different languages. It is the same today when we receive the baptism of the Holy spirit and we speaks in tongues and pray with supernatural power.

This book will renew, energize, and awaken your spirit to accept the Spirit's power that will help you to live a holy, healthy, and godly life as a child of God. You will be able to do impossible things that you cannot imagine through the power of the Holy Spirit's supernatural power.

This Book will help you to know that God continues to pour out His Spirit, just as on the day of Pentecost, to those who abide and believe in His Son Jesus Christ our Savior Lord, with obedience to the Word of God in order to receive the gift of eternal life through the power of the Holy Spirit.

*The Spirit Power* is a book that will help you to begin a new life in Christ. Salvation is the gift of Grace with abundant life that the Spirit Power offers. May our Lord and Savior continue to pour out His Spirit on all those who believe in Him.

Prayer: May He let this book bring unbelievers to Christ's feet on the throne of grace. All other religions of the earth will know and worship the true God, the King of kings, the Lord of lords and the God of gods. May every soul of human beings worship, praise, and glorify Him where He sits at the right hand of God the Father.

*The Spirit Power* is an inspirational book and the right book for you. It will lift up your spirit to be in tune with the Spirit of the Almighty God—Father, Son, and Holy Spirit forever one God.

Amen, amen, and amen.

# 1

# Faithfulness

Faithfulness extends from growing in a relationship with God to growing in relationships with others. It means fellowship and developing friendships with other believers.

Faithfulness produces deep assurances that make us connected to God with a bond of perfection that cannot be broken and that will extend into eternity. God's faithfulness to us in this world, through our Lord Jesus Christ, leads us to faithfulness to Him and other people around us.

For God so loved the world that he gave his only begotten Son. God the father calls us, even when we are in sin and trespass against Him, into fellowship with His Son Jesus Christ our Lord. Faithfulness stands at the heart of who God is and what He wants to do through us, which is based on our commitment and trust.

Our faith will help us to trust in the Lord. The Holy Spirit will continue to produce the fruit of faith in us, so that when we make a promise to go to Church, we will go. When we make a commitment we will honor it. We will be consistent and reliable, and prove, with all of our strength, every aspect of our faithfulness.

Faithfulness means that we will be able to carry out all of our efforts faithfully and to give our best to the Lord in our relationship with him. All believers in Christ must be faithful in all areas of their lives, whether in little things or big things.

Faithfulness means keeping our promises, getting to work on time, doing our best in our jobs, being faithful to our fellow coworkers, managers, and supervisors around us, being faithful to our spouses, friends, and relatives, and being especially faithful to our children and grandchildren.

We must remain faithful by making good decisions that will help them in any particular situation or circumstances and seeking the good of others in our decision-making, at all times.

Believers do their best in working for the glory of God, not for the praise of any human being. They know that their entire job is a divine appointment is from God. It is doing God's work, achieving God's purpose in our lives and being faithful.

As believers bear this fruit of the Spirit, faithfulness, God will be able to produce more and more fruits in us. Believers will experience decreases in faithfulness to God if they stop reading the Word of God, or stop living in a close and good relationship with the Lord. They will also find that they begin to spend less and less time in prayer and that their faith will begin to shake.

Faithfulness is one of the most important fruits of the Spirit that no believer should neglect. And the Lord said, "If ye had faith as a grain of mustard seed, ye shall say unto this sycamine tree, be thou plucked up by the root, and be thou planted in the sea; and it should obey you." Luke 17:6.

As a mustard seed, means that if we trust God with all our problems and if we pray to him with faith, He will answer that prayer, if it is according to His will. He will grant our requests according to His riches in glory. Believers must take their minds off of themselves, their parents, husbands and wives, children, and off of any circumstances, and focus completely on the Lord, the author and finisher of our faith.

We need to see Jesus and what He has done for us and through us for other people. Through the power of the cross and through the power of the Holy Spirit, we are healed. By reading the Word of God, we are increasing our faith everyday and continuing our fellowship with Him.

"So then faith cometh by hearing, and hearing, and hearing by the Word of God." Rom. 10:17. By entering the truth of the Word of God into our heart, we increase our faith. Believers must combine their faith with the faith of others by sharing, maintaining fellowship with God, teaching, learning, conducting Bible studies, and teaching others about what God says in so many areas, such as believing, miracles, healing, provisions and divine appointment for the children of God.

Believers must be doers of the Word of God, not hearers alone, follow God's commandment through His word, and maintain intimate relationships with the Lord until the Word of God stays in their hearts permanently.

"For verily I say to you, That whosoever shall say to this mountain, Be you removed and be you cast into the sea and shall not doubt in his heart but shall believe that those things which he says shall come to pass; he shall have whatsoever he says. Therefore, I say to you; what things so ever you desire, when you pray, believe that you receive them, and you shall have them." Mark 11:23-24.

The Holy Spirit produces the fruit of faith with the love of God in our hearts. "But without faith it is impossible to please him. For he that cometh to God must believe that he is and that he is a rewarder of them that diligently seek him." Heb. 11:6.

In the midst of temptation, He remains faithful as He fulfills His promises. Apostle Paul stated that even we are faithless, "But as God is true, our word toward you was not yea and nay. For the Son of God, Jesus Christ, who was preached among you by us, even by me and Silvanus and Timotheus, was not yea and nay, but in Him was yes." 2 Cor. 1:18-19.

God remains faithful and true. God remains faithful to New Testament believers by fulfilling all of the promises in the Old Testament. In the Old Testament, God's faithfulness and his covenant love were closely related, "Know therefore that the Lord thy God, he is God the faithful God, which keepeth covenant and mercy with them that love him and keep his commandments to a thousand generations." Deut. 7:9.

The most profound example of faithfulness is the bond between God and the people of Israel. Even though the people of Israel were unfaithful to God, God let them know that He is married to them in faithfulness and that they must acknowledge the Lord. "I will even betroth thee unto me in faithfulness; and thou shalt know the Lord." Hos. 2:20.

God was looking for righteousness, justice, steadfast, love, kindness, and faithfulness in His people. In the same way, He wants us to demonstrate faithfulness to him and sincere, love, and compassion for others.

The Israelites were expected to respond with faithfulness to God, because He had acted faithfully to them through the covenant. King David, Joseph, Abraham, and other godly people in the Old Testament, chose to walk the ways of faithfulness and truth. Just as God is faithful, those who believe in Him should exhibit faithfulness and love in their lives.

In the New Testament, God acts with faithfulness; He provides for both just and unjust people and rewards those who follow His commandments. "That thine alms may be in secret: and thy Father which seeth in secret himself shall reward thee openly. But thou, when thou prayest, enter into thy closet, and when thou has shut thy door, pray to thy Father which is in secret; and thy Father which seeth in secret shall reward thee openly." Matt. 6:4, 6.

He provides a means of escape in the midst of temptation. "There hath no temptation taken you but such as is common to man: but God is faithful, who will not suffer you to be tempted above that ye are able; but will with the temptation also make a way of escape, that ye may be able to bear it."1 Cor. 10:13.

Apostle Paul stated that even when we are faithless, God remains faithful and true. God remains faithful to New Testament believers by fulfilling all of the promises in the Old Testament. Christians must respond to God in faithfulness. An example of the faithfulness of New Testament believers is that of Epaphras and Tychicus, both of whom were identified as faithful ministers of Christ, "As ye also learned of Epaphras our dear fellow servant, who is for you a faithful minister of Christ; All my state shall Tychicus declare unto you, who is a beloved brother, and a faithful minister and fellow servant in the Lord." Col. 1:7, 4:7.

Apostle Paul remained faithful to God, in spite of tremendous pressures. Timothy selected teachers who would exhibit faithfulness, one of the most outstanding characteristics of Christians. The Holy Spirit of God enables Christians to remain faithful to God and other believers, as well as to nonbelievers.

Believers must spend more time praising, thanking, confessing our past, present, and future sins to God, and listening to Him through His word. Faithfulness involves a desire to know God's truth and striving to grow in our understanding of God's purposes for our lives.

Faithfulness Stretches you from growing in a good relationship with God, to growing in a good relationship with others, believers and non-believers. Faithfulness means being full of faith, strong or very firm in one's belief, loyal and constant in the performance of duties or services, true to one's work, reliable, and dependable.

God is the only one who has always been and will always be faithful to us; he never changes and he will never change. God is always faithful to us, even when we are unfaithful. God always helps us through difficult times and through pleasure. God is always there for us.

God is faithful to us because He gave us His only Son our Lord Jesus Christ who paid the price, with His own blood, for our past, present and future sins.

God's faithfulness does not depend on what we do or don't do. God is faithful to all believers and unbelievers, to the just and unjust. Faithfulness is one of the most important aspects of the Spirit that helps all believers in Christ to grow in their walk with the Lord. Faithfulness is committing oneself to something, or someone.

For example, a faithful believer requires a personal relationship with the Lord and must not wander away from His commitment or promises to the Lord. We must be faithful and trust in God. Prophet Isaiah stated, "O Lord, thou art my God; I will exalt thee, I will praise thy name; for thou has done wonderful things, thy counsels of old are faithfulness and truth." Isa. 25:1.

Paul prays, "That he would grant you, according to the riches of his glory, to be strengthened with might by his Spirit in the inner man; That Christ may dwell in your hearts by faith, that ye, being rooted and grounded with love." Eph. 3:16-17.

Christ dwells in our hearts through the power of the Holy Spirit and he produces all of the fruits of the Spirit within us, so that we can be examples of true Christians and share His love with those who do not know Him. The key and most important tool to having all the fruits of the Holy Spirit produced in us, is the Word of God that abides in us forever. Believers must learn how to stay in the Word of God and to eat the Word of God, as someone eats candy or drinks water.

"He that is faithful in that which is least is faithful also in much: and he that is unjust in the least is unjust also in much. Therefore, ye have not been faithful in the unrighteous mammon, who will commit to your trust the true riches?

And if ye have not been faithful in that which is another man's, who shall give you that which is your own." Luke 16:10-12. Believers must ask God for spiritual strength in order that, when our Lord and Savior establishes His kingdom upon His return to earth on His second coming, all those who believe in Him may participate with Christ in His future kingdom.

We believers must ask God to strengthen us through the power of the Holy Spirit that we may be able to faithfully carry out their obligation to the righteous towards both God and our fellow man.

Believers must maintain strong faith in the Lord by simply having faith in Him and trusting Him. "But without faith it is impossible to please him: for he that cometh to God must believe that He is and that He is a rewarder of them that diligently seek Him." Heb. 11:6.

Also, "For by grace are ye saved through faith; and that not yourselves; it is the gift of God." Eph. 2:8.

# 2

# Gentleness

Gentleness is not something we can achieve through our own efforts; we must rely upon our Lord and Savior to help us so that we may respond to earthly troubles with gentleness, tenderness, and quiet spirits. John 16:13.

One the greatest blessings of the fruit of gentleness is that it takes us from the burden of self-defense and self-promotion, to understanding how many people strive to prove themselves to other people.

Believers must yield all authority and glory to God, stand before Him in humility, surrender all to him, and stand in position to do his bidding at all times. Gentleness is not something we can achieve on our own.

We must rely upon the Lord to help us respond to all of life's afflictions with gentleness, tenderness, and a quiet spirit. Gentleness is a great blessing that frees us from the burdens of selfishness, self-defense, and self-promotion. Some people continue to build themselves up in order to gain approval or praise from people.

They are struggling to move themselves to high positions, where people will look at them with high hopes, or they are competing with other people around them. Whereas, we see a godly person who yields all honors, all glory, all dominion, all power to God, in the Spirit of submission.

Believers must yield all authority, glory, and power to God, stand before him in humility, be ready to follow His commands at all times, and always be ready to help others who are in need of help. Let us totally give ourselves to Christ and receive the strength that will develop the Spirit of humility and meekness in us, to be able to understand the true meaning of gentleness.

We must try our best to let our gentleness be known to all. The Lord is near, and the time is now. Gentleness is the same as meekness. A believer with the fruit of gentleness has compassion to control what is not going well in his life and the lives of others.

A gentle person always has things under control; a gentle fruit believer will always correct wrongs and have the power of the Spirit and strength to function in any situation. Paul stated, "Be completely humble and gentle; be patient, bearing with one another with love." Eph. 4:2.

People with gentle spirits always care for others and always bring injustice to light so that it can be corrected. Believers with the fruit of the Spirit of gentleness possess more strength under the control of the Holy Spirit.

Gentleness has never been a sign of weakness in the life of a true Christian; it has always been exercising power and control in a gentle manner that comes from God. God is the God of power, might and love. "Take my yoke upon you and learn of me; for I am meek and lowly in heart for my yoke is easy, and my burden is light, and ye shall find rest unto your soul." Matt. 11:29.

"And the servant of the Lord must not strive; but be gentle unto all men, apt to teach and patient." 2 Tim. 2:24. Our Lord emphasized that we will have a just and good Spirit towards others if we approach them with the Spirit of gentleness.

Apostle Paul reminded the people in Thessalonica that he was gentle among them and treated them as a nursing mother cherishes her new born baby, "But we are gentle among you, even as a nurse cherisheth her children: So being affectionately desirous of you, but also our own souls. Because ye were dear unto us."1 Thes. 2:7-8.

With these words of the Scriptures, it shows that God does not want any believers, His children, to treat their fellow human beings badly. God's nature is to be merciful, kind, and gentle towards people, especially the people who are in the world. Believers must be an example for them, so that they can be converted when they see our gentle character revealed in everything we do.

Apostle Peter, in his epistle, encourages women to be the hidden person of the heart, with the incorruptible beauty of a gentle and quiet Spirit, which is very precious in the sight of God. "But let it be the hidden man of the heart, that which is not corruptible even the ornament of a meek and quiet, which is in the sight of God of great price." 1 Pet. 3:4.

Apostle James emphasizes to us that, "But the wisdom that is from above is first pure, them peaceable, gentle, and easy to be treated, full of mercy and good fruits, without partiality, and without hypocrisy." Jas. 3:17.

Believers must learn to exercise and express a genuine love for others around them to believers and non-believers with the fruit of heavenly wisdom from above in a pure, peaceable, gentle, and kind manner.

# 3

# Self-Control

God holds individuals responsible for their own actions. It is fundamentally important and an integral part of Christianity that an individual who is entrusted with the care of others must be able to govern himself properly.

Self-control is the same as temperance; it means exercising power over oneself, having self-mastery over our passions, controlling our thoughts, and regulating our conduct, without being duly swayed through desires.

Lust, greed, gluttony, alcoholism, conceit, sexual sins, gossiping, violence, quarreling, and false and reckless speech are just a few of many sins that a believer may commit if he or she does not have the fruit of the Spirit of self-control.

Self-control is for the benefit of the believer who exercises it, but others can still follow in the believer's footsteps in order to exercise self-control in their lives. Self-control provides the ability to resist what may damage or cause pain to other people around us. Therefore, believers must exercise self-control on behalf of other people and themselves.

Paul stated that, "But I keep under my body, and bring it into subjection: lest that by any means, when I have preached to others, I myself should be a castaway." 1 Cor. 9:27.

A lack of self-control shows shortsightedness because its damage is long lasting, affecting our future both physically and spiritually. Apostle Paul advised or instructed single people in the Church to get married, including young widows, if they could not stay clean, so that they would not fall into temptation and the sin of sexual immorality.

Self-control is God's manifestation of the work of the Holy Spirit in the lives of believers. Christians can have self-control because of the power of the indwelling of the Holy Spirit. The Spirit of God controls the minds of believers and continues to strengthen them with power. The flesh and the Spirit are contrary to one another.

Self-control through the Holy Spirit is not a daily discipline; it is a fruit of the Spirit. It is not a list of rules, but a guiding principle that comes from the Spirit. It means behavior focused on doing the will of God and the will of God alone.

By totally surrendering ourselves to God's control, the spiritual fruit of self-control will come. We cannot master our own lives; this can only be done by the power of the Holy Spirit. The Holy Spirit of God will help us to control, respond, yield, and surrender to the will of God.

Self-control is not gained through suppression alone, but also by controlling the lusts of the flesh. Those who are led by the Spirit, live in the Spirit, and walk in the Spirit are able to attain self-control and are on their way fruitful growth in God's character.

Gluttony affects our characters in all areas of self-control, exhausting us of perseverance for good and draining us of our resistance to evil. Many lack resistance if they cannot leave food or alcohol alone.

They are unable to say no to a lot of things, especially in restaurants where people serve themselves and they can eat all they want to for a standard price. This type of lack of self-control is contrary to what God desires from His children.

God considers a gluttonous character as unloving and evil; if the person loved himself, he would not continue eating too much until falling sick or out of shape. "And after certain days, when Felix came with his wife Drusilla, which was a Jewess, he sent for Paul, and heard him concerning the faith in Christ.

And as he reasoned of righteousness, temperance, and judgment to come, Felix trembled, and answered, Go thy way for this time; when I have a convenient season, I will call for thee." Acts 24:24-25.

Paul mentioned self-control, one of the fruits of the Spirit, as one of the most important parts of his faith in Christ, when he was speaking to the Roman Governor of Judea. Paul also mentioned the importance of righteousness and judgment.

Believers must pray and ask the Holy Spirit to help them to control their human nature, transforming their thinking, thoughts, and perspective in accordance with the Spirit's empowerment so that they may exercise self-control and live by the teachings and control of the Holy Scriptures.

"For what the law could not do, in that it was weak through the flesh, God sending His own Son in the likeness of sinful flesh, and for sin, condemned sin in the flesh: That the righteousness of the law might be fulfilled in us, who walk not after the flesh, but after the Spirit." Rom. 8:3-4.

"For we know that the Law is spiritual, but I am carnal, sold under sin. For that which I do I allow not: for what I would, that do I not; but what I hate, that do I. If then I do that which I would not, I consent unto the law that it is good. Now then it is no more I that do it, but sin that dwelleth in me." Rom. 7: 14-17.

Apostle Paul explained his own life experience to us so that we could have an understanding of sin, which must be defined by the law of God. It is not enough to overpower the control, pull, and deception of our human nature.

Paul made this clear and precise: that knowing God's law cannot solve the problem of our sinful nature. Even though God's law gives us knowledge of sin, we still need the empowerment of the Holy Spirit to help us exercise self-control.

Knowledge of sin is essential to our spiritual growth. We must also practice the fruit of the Spirit of righteousness. However, this is directly due to the weakness of our flesh, we cannot attain true righteousness by our own power.

Rather, only by changing our sinful nature to God's divine nature can we overcome sin. We need the Spirit of Jesus Christ our Savior and Lord living inside of us, indwelling us, and sealing us, just as Apostle Paul said, "I have been crucified with Christ: nevertheless I live; ye not I, but Christ liveth in me: and the life which I now live in the flesh I live by the faith of the Son of God, who loved me, and gave himself for me." Gal. 2:20.

Believers must be delivered from themselves and made righteous, so that they may produce the fruit of the Spirit in abundance. The fruit of the Spirit must reflect the fruits of goodness, faithfulness, and self-control, inherent in God's nature.

If God's Spirit is in us, these inherited characteristics that are the fruits of the Spirit should also become fundamental characteristics of all believers' natures, that is, as long as we remain in Christ and continue to serve God from our heart. Apostle Peter summarizes these by saying to all believers in Jesus Christ,

"And beside this, giving all diligence, add to your faith virtue; and virtue knowledge, and to knowledge temperance; and to temperance; patience; and to patience godliness; and to godliness brotherly kindness; and to brotherly kindness charity.

"For if these things be in you, and abound, they make you that ye shall neither be barren nor unfruitful in the knowledge of our Lord Jesus Christ. But he that lacketh these and hath forgotten that he was purged from his old sins.

"Wherefore the rather, brethren, give diligence to make your calling and election sure: for if ye do these things, ye shall never fall: For so an entrance shall be ministered unto you abundantly into the everlasting kingdom of our Lord and Savior Jesus Christ." 2 Pet. 1:5-11.

Apostle Peter explained how important our spiritual growth is to maintaining our spirit in an obedient relationship with our Lord now on earth and in our inheritance of eternal life in heaven.

Believers must acquire great abilities to remain spiritually strong and active, which depends on how much hope we have and how much we rely on God's power. When we live in Spirit-filled obedience to what the Scripture commands or instructs, we will continue to echo and re-echo it through our lives.

"A kind man benefits himself." Prov. 11:17. Kindness open doors for service. For example, Barnabas, called the son of encouragement, during the apostolic era, sold his land and gave the money for the work of the Gospel's ministry. Acts of kindness were exhibited throughout Barnabas' ministry in service of the Lord. "Gentle answer turn away wrath." Prov. 15:1.

Kindness also softens the hard and angry hearts of the people around us. The self-control fruit of the Spirit must yield control to God. We must feed our soul daily with God's Word; we must rely on the Holy Spirit's connecting power; it is the fruit of the Spirit that comes from the Spirit. It is a guiding principal that means focusing on doing the will of God.

Believers must be sensitive to the ways in which he might convict us of what we choose and what actions we take. The more we move ourselves under the God's commands and His plan, the more we will lead a focused, disciplined, and purposeful life.

It is a lifelong process that every believer in Jesus Christ must follow. Self-control through the Holy Spirit is not a one-time practice. Self-control is one of the fruits of the Spirit in believers' lives, which means that believers have ability, command, mastery, possession, and control of their behavior in all things, no matter what.

Peter says, "Make every effort to add to your faith goodness, and to goodness, knowledge, and to knowledge self-Control and to Self-Control, perseverance, and to perseverance, godliness, and to godliness, mutual affection, and to mutual affection, love." 2 Pet. 1:5-7.

Christians must possess the fruit of self-control in order to be free from all or any form of temptation that comes in the way of individual believers in Jesus Christ. Christians must be able to have control over the food they eat; to be able to control food, not letting food control them and make them sick to the point of untimely death.

Believers must exercise self-control over their finances in order to be able to save for rainy days or for unforeseen circumstances.

Believers must be able to exercise self-control when faced with material things of this world and think of how to help others instead of buying houses, diamonds, jewelry in excess, and storing them in the safe deposit boxes and banks, where they will even pay money every month to keep them there.

Believers must be able to have self-control over family problems between spouses, siblings, and children, and over problems in the office with supervisors and managers, in the government with high ranking officials, and with Church believers.

Believers must be able to exercise self-control over their anger and anything that could upset them. Believers must exercise self-control over how many and what types of friends they keep, who they are and what their relationship is like with the Lord, what type of influences they have, and whether they can grow in the Lord during their friendship.

Believers must have self-control through the help of the Holy Spirit; this can never be done without the indwelling power of the Holy Spirit working in us and controlling our lives.

Believers must be able to yield to the Holy Spirit's direction in order to possess the spirit of self-control from wine, excess of food, and from any earthly thing that can cause so many problems.

When Jesus washed the feet of the disciples, "After that he poureth water into a basin, and began to wash the disciples' feet, and to wipe them with the towel wherewith he was girded." John 13:5.

Self-control means literally keeping oneself away from such things as alcohol, sex, and drugs. People's lives must be lives of discipline; everything must be taken in moderation, as believers live in close communion and close relationships with the Lord and are obedient to His commandments each day of their lives.

The Holy Spirit works wonderful miracles; the Spirit transforms believers into the likeness of Jesus Christ. They become like Him by beholding Him. Just as the branch derives all its life and nourishment from the vine, in the same way, believers in Christ derive their strength from the true vine and thus live faithful, fruitful lives for God.

The most important goal of believers is to be obedient to Christ's commandments in order to be able to abide in Him. To abide in Christ is to live in the Spirit. This means abiding in Christ and the Spirit empowering, so that we can live a life of obedience to His commandments and to His instructions.

# 4

# Longsuffering

Longsuffering is the fruit of the Spirit that is the result of receiving the teaching of the Holy Spirit into one's heart.

Longsuffering is the opposite of anger. It does not surrender to any situation or succumb under pressure. Longsuffering is the same as forbearance, patience, and self-restraint; it does not retaliate or punish those who do us wrong.

God demonstrated His own longsuffering to us by showing us His love. An example of God's longsuffering toward men occurred during the flood. He gave Noah one hundred twenty years to enter the boat. He gave the people of Noah's day one hundred twenty years to repent from their sins.

Other examples include those of Sodom and Gomorrah and the rebellion of the children of Israel in the wilderness. All believers must go through longsuffering in order to develop a sense of maturity, knowledge, and understanding of the way of God.

Longsuffering is a very important fruit of the Spirit that is necessary for the people of God to be able to get along where there are differences or problems in the Church or community. Longsuffering is very essential in order to live a life that is pleasing to God; it is also essential for living a happy and godly life.

Longsuffering is a fruit of the Spirit. Longsuffering is similar and the same as patience and forbearance; longsuffering is self-restraint in the face of provocation. A person who is longsuffering is not quick to retaliate or promptly punish someone who has insulted, offended, or harmed him or her. It is the opposite of anger; it is intimately associated with mercy.

Longsuffering is an attribute of God and, thus, a fruit of the Spirit. God's longsuffering is revealed, "And the Lord passed by before him, and proclaimed, The Lord, The Lord God, merciful and gracious, longsuffering, and abundant in goodness and truth." Exo. 34:6.

"The Lord is longsuffering, and of great mercy, forgiving iniquity and transgression, and by no means clearing the guilty. Visiting the iniquity of the fathers upon the children unto the third and fourth generation." Num. 14:18.

"In the day of my trouble I will call upon thee: for thou will answer me." Psl. 86:16. "Or despises thou the riches of his goodness and forbearance and longsuffering; not knowing that the goodness of God leadeth thee to repentance?" Rom. 2:4.

"The Lord is not slack concerning his promise, as some men count slackness; but is longsuffering to usward, not willing that any should perish, but that all should come to repentance." 2 Pet. 3:9.

God's longsuffering delays His wrath, "What if God, willing to shew his wrath, and to make his power known, endured with much longsuffering the vessels of wrath fitted to destruction." Rom. 9:22.

"For Christ also hath once suffered for sins, the just for the unjust, that he might bring us to God, being put to death in the flesh, but quickened by the Spirit." 1 Pet. 3:18.

Christ's patience and endurance in His handling of sinners demonstrates His longsuffering. God promises that He will exercise long-temperance with us as we repent and dedicate ourselves to obedience and service of God.

Jesus Christ sets the standard of longsuffering. Many believers, God's servants, develop the quality of longsuffering through their service and dedication to the Lord. Having been elected by God, believers must clothe themselves with longsuffering. A minister of God must encourage, rebuke, love, and not only correct with love, but also with longsuffering.

# 5

# Obedience

We have to notice the sequence of events in this record of the outpouring of the Spirit on Samaritan believers. Philip preached the Gospel of the kingdom and God confirmed his words with miraculous signs.

Many Samaritans received the Word of God, believed in Jesus Christ, were baptized in water, and experienced salvation in the regenerative work of the Holy Spirit and the power of the Kingdom of God.

The Holy Spirit, however, had not yet come upon any of them after their conversion to Christ and their water baptism. The Samaritans fully met the conditions for salvation; they were Christians before the Spirit came upon them.

The believers were baptized. This shows clearly that the faith of the Samaritans was genuine and faithful. The Samaritans committed themselves to Christ through water baptism, supporting Philip's belief that they had believed in Christ's salvation.

These actions by the Samaritan show love and obedience, which lead to regeneration and the indwelling of the Holy Spirit. "Then Philip began with that very passage of scripture and told him the good news about Jesus. As they travel along the road, they came to some water and the Eunuch said,

"Look, here is water, why should I be baptized? And he gave orders to stop the chariot, Then both Philip and the Eunuch went down into the water and Philip baptized him." Acts 8:35-38.

We can see the supernatural experience before and after water baptism; believers walk with the Spirit and, being led by Him, are always filled with the Spirit. "Ye became followers of us, and of the Lord, having received the word in much affliction, with joy of the Holy Ghost." 1 Thes. 1:6.

Apostle Paul told believers that they are those who imitate Christ, endure suffering with the joy given by the Holy Spirit, and are models of faith and righteousness. We cannot gather or store away the power of the Holy Spirit; instead, we experience God's power when we totally surrender to Him, so that He can use us. God the Father releases His power to us through the Holy Spirit, the fruit of the Spirit.

God's power is the only power that can enable us to exhibit the fruit of the Spirit, which reveals Christ-like character in the lives of believers. The power of the Holy Spirit is for all believers; it is available to every believer who willingly surrenders all and lives moment by moment in submission and obedience to the direction of the Holy Spirit.

The Spirit Power is the divine power of energy that God is willing to direct in and through all believers; it is also the divine authority of the Word of God, needed to carry out the work of God the Father, God the Son, and God the Holy Spirit has assigned to us.

It is His power through us that inspires us and carries out the work in us. "Abraham believed the Lord, and he was credited it to him as righteousness." Gen. 15:6. Abram had faith in God and he loved the Lord. He stood firm on the Word of God.

Abram committed his life to the Lord, and to hearing and following God's instructions and obeying the Lord. God saw Abram's heart of faith and credited it to him as righteousness. Abram was living in a correct relationship with God and his will for him.

God entered into covenant of fellowship with Abram, whereby Abram received God as his shield, as well as the reward of many offspring and the promise of land. Abram rejoiced in the Lord because of his obedience to God's instructions.

Under the new covenant, God's blessings and a correct relationship and fellowship with Him also come through faith. Listening to the Holy Spirit is much more difficult than obeying the letter of the law, because we will have to stop listening to ourselves, and start listening to God. We might have to get free of some of the traps of the Law such as self-righteousness or self-pity.

Obeying the law leads us to either to self-righteousness or to the other extreme of constant guilt. God does not want believers to live self-righteous lives; He wants us to follow and listen to the Spirit so that we can produce good fruit in our lives and so that others around us might follow the same steps of obedience.

"I no longer count on my own righteousness through obeying the Law; rather, I become righteous through faith in Christ. For God's way of making us right with himself depends on faith." Php. 3:9.

The righteousness of believers consists first in being forgiven, justified, and accepted by God as a gift received through faith; however, God's Word states that our righteousness is also Christ's righteousness Jesus Himself, living within our hearts.

Therefore, the righteousness we have is not of ourselves but of Jesus Christ, in whom we put our faith; through the indwelling, we become one in Him.

The basis of our salvation and our hope of righteousness is the sacrificial death and shed blood of Christ. Faithfulness leads to obedience, and obedience brings about rich blessings from the Lord.

The Bible tells us that, "A faithful man will be richly blessed." Prov. 28:20. To obey or not to obey the

Lord God this has been and is the question for every human being. Obedience, as opposed to disobedience, is a life and death issue.

God has given humankind the power of choice. The choice of obedience leads to God's promised blessing of life; the choice of disobedience leads to curses, judgment, and death.

God's clear instructions to the very first human beings in the Garden of Eden were to refrain from eating the fruit of the tree of knowledge of good and evil. God tested and expected their obedience. They disobeyed, thereby losing initial favor with God and becoming spiritually dead.

The obedience of Abram is the most exemplary in the Old Testament. On two occasions, Abram demonstrated total submission to God's commandments. Abram obeyed God's command to leave His father's home in the land of Chaldees, which was beautiful, civilized, and well developed during those years, to go to an unknown place, where he had never lived before, by going to the land of Canaan.

Abram's obedience resulted in his being elected a chosen one with a special role in God's plan of salvation for humankind. Second, he obeyed God's command to offer his son Isaac as a sacrifice. Gen. 22:1-19. Obedience was the main concern during the time of Israelites in the wilderness. God chose Moses to direct the Israelites.

Those who were in this special relationship with God received the Ten Commandments for moral and religious guidance. Obedience underlies two or more key verses of the Pentateuch.

One of them is: "Be holy because I, the Lord your God, am holy." Lev. 19:2. Obedience should come and originate from a commitment to living a holy life before God and others in the covenant community.

A divine call, with total love for God, results in unhesitating obedience to God's will. Our Lord Jesus was the supreme example of obedience to the heavenly Father when He gave Himself as the ultimate sacrifice for the atonement of our sins.

Jesus prayed for the disciples to be sanctified and made holy, so that they could live holy lives inwardly and outwardly. Inner holiness and cleansing are required for obedience. The Holy Spirit is provided to all who believe in Jesus Christ. The Spirit's abiding presence enables all of God's people to carry out God's will and learn to live obediently before God.

# 6

# Perseverance

God often used the fruit of the Spirit, perseverance, to highlight the contrast between the mutability of human beings and the world.

The idea is to exercise energetically resistance, steadfastness under pressure, and endurance in the face of trials. Perseverance or endurance, faith, and hope are emphasized in the Old Testament, and they mean waiting for or expecting.

All believers must persevere in order to be able to personally attain the ultimate salvation of God. Sometimes perseverance can be seen as confidence in whatever believers in Christ are doing, or as their expectations, with the power of faithfulness in God, who is our deliverer.

The Psalm of David says, "For evil doers shall be cut off, but those that wait upon the Lord, they shall inherit the earth." Psl. 37:9. Perseverance can also be seen as a believer's strong hope in the Lord. Another

Psalm of David says, "But let those that put their trust in thee rejoice; let them also that love thy name be joyful in thee." Psl. 5:55.

The book of Zephaniah says, "Therefore wait ye upon me, said the Lord, until the day that I rise up to the prey: for my determination is to gather the nations, that I may assemble the kingdoms, fierce anger: for all the earth shall be devoured with the fire of my jealousy." Zeph. 3:8.

We also have to look to Micah, "Therefore I will look unto the Lord, I will wait for the God of my salvation: my God will hear me." Mic. 7:7. We need to review the Old Testament for how people persevered under trials.

Prophet Micah, in the middle of a morally disobedient society, put his faith in the Lord and his promises. He was confident that God would sustain him and bring judgment against all the evildoers. Righteousness will reign in the heart of all believers in Jesus Christ.

Christ has offered the gift of salvation to all who put their faith in Him. Zephaniah turned to God's plan to redeem the nations after they have been purified through judgment.

He believed that the nations would someday be reconciled to God, that the people of God would call and God would answer and fulfill their hearts' desires, and that Christ would rule over the nations. Abraham persevered despite temptations.

The same was the case of Isaac, Noah, and all of the prophets; they stood fast, not shakily, in the Lord. The main goal of perseverance or endurance is for faith and hope to be emphasized. Believers need to persevere in order to personally attain to the ultimate salvation of God.

Perseverance can be seen through good works, "Truly the signs of an apostle were wrought among you in all patience, in signs, and wonders, and mighty deed." 2 Cor. 12:12. Perseverance, which is one of the fruits of the Holy Spirit's product, can also be seen through suffering.

"So that we ourselves glory in you in the Churches of God, that ye may be counted worthy of the kingdom of God, for which ye also suffer." 2 Thes. 1:4. Believers in Thessalonica persevered in faith through persecution, even though they were going through persecution and trials.

They believed that God would make them worthy of His grace and His kingdom. The lives of Thessalonian believers were marked by perseverance and faith; they suffered at the hands of unbelievers and went through many trials, but they persevered in faith and were counted worthy of the kingdom of God for whom they suffered.

Apostle James referred to Job's perseverance in his writing and said, "Behold, we count them happy, which endure. Ye have heard of the patience of Job, and have seen the end of the Lord; that the Lord is very pitiful and tender mercy." Jas. 5:11.

We see Job's perseverance and endurance throughout his trial, during which he did not lose faith in God. Faith triumphs to the very end in the middle of sufferings. In the end, it was clear that God cared about Job and He sustained him with His mercy and love.

James wants believers to know that God cares and is concerned about all of His people. He has seen their suffering and He wants them to turn to him. He will sustain them with His great compassion, mercy, and love.

Perseverance is one of the fruits of the Holy Spirit that all believers in Jesus Christ must allow the Holy Spirit to produce within them.

Perseverance and faith are inseparable both are connected and necessary in the service of the Lord and in the lives of all believers. The Book of Hebrews says that Moses persevered in the face of the Egyptian King, "By faith he forsook Egypt, not fearing the wrath of the king: for he endured, as seen him who is invisible." Heb. 11:27.

Moses was full of the Spirit of God and envisioned what was going to take place. Moses saw He who is invisible, through faith. We also have to look at the letter in the book of Revelation where our Lord gave His word of assurance to all believers and said that He is aware of their perseverance.

"I know thy works, and thy labor, and thy patience, and how thou canst not bear them which are evil, and thou hast tried them which say they are apostles, and are not; and hast found them liars; and hast borne, and hast patience, and for my name's sake hast labored, and hast not fainted." Rev. 2:2-3.

This is one of the major concerns that our Lord mentioned in His final message to the Seven Churches - it concerns the teachers and pastors who change the Word of God and cause weakness to the power and authority of the Word of God. Christ informs all Churches to be aware and make sure they test all who claim to be spiritual in the Word of God.

They must stand fast and immovable in times of threats and hardship. They must be steadfast with endurance during trials and perseverance during tribulations. Believers must persevere in order to receive God's blessings that He promised to those who believe in Him.

All servants of the Lord need perseverance. It is a moral commitment and effort. It must involve doing the will of God; it is also a tool for being eligible for receiving the salvation that God has promised.

Believers must persevere, fixing their eye, spirit, soul, and body on Jesus Christ who is the supreme model of perseverance. He is the one through whom the Holy Spirit will give us all that we need to persevere in His service. God the Father has blessed us with the gift of grace and everlasting life through faith, in order for all believers to grow in spiritual maturity for the salvation of God.

The Holy Spirit will continue to produce the fruit of perseverance. The Spirit of God will uphold us, enable us, nurture our faith, and strengthen us in the hopes of receiving His inheritance, which He has prepared for all those who love Him.

The gift of eternal life follows the Holy Spirit's energizing through the fruit of perseverance. All believers in Jesus Christ must be filled with the fruit of the Holy Spirit called perseverance, which is the same as endurance.

# 7

# Forgiveness

The fruit of the Holy Spirit's work in the lives of individual Christians results in active love for God and others, rejoicing in all kinds of circumstances, peacefulness, kindness, goodness, the will to freely help others, and the ability to live a self-controlled life.

The fruits are the evidence and result of Spirit-filled, sanctified life. All Christians should receive the gifts of the Spirit according to Christ's commandments.

All Christians must use the gifts that the Holy Spirit gave them lovingly, joyfully, peacefully, patiently, and kindly, in keeping with the other fruits of the Spirit. The fruit of the Spirit is the result of the Holy Spirit's presence and work in the lives of maturing believers.

Forgiveness is one of the itemized fruits of the Spirit: God removes sinners' sins permanently through it. Forgiveness is to forgive offences against God's holiness. Forgiveness can be extended from individuals to entire nations for example, the nation of Israel. God forgave Israel of its sins again and again in the Old Testament.

God is merciful and righteous in His ways. God forgives a repentant heart and restores individuals or nations. He did not bring punishment unto Israel as He had planned to do. He wanted to bring judgment on the city of Nineveh, but He was merciful and compassionate. He sent Jonah to correct them and the entire people of Nineveh repented and changed.

In the New Testament, forgiveness and spiritual transformation became reality through the appearance, death, resurrection, and ascension of our Lord Jesus Christ at the right hand of God. Forgiveness extended to individual Gentiles.

Christ preached and proclaimed the kingdom of God, and told people to repent so that they could enter the kingdom of God. Christ is a mediator of a new covenant, offered for salvation after repentance and forgiveness.

"And, behold, certain of the scribes said within themselves, this man blasphemeth. And Jesus knowing their thoughts said, wherefore think ye evil in your heart? For whether is easier, to say, thy sins be forgiven thee, or to say, Arise, and walk? But that ye may know that the Son of Man hath power on earth to forgive sins, then saith he to the sick of the palsy Arise, take up thy bed, and go unto thine house." Matt. 9:3-6.

Jesus showed the Scribes that He had authority on earth to forgive sin. When the people saw what had happened they gave glory to God for giving such power to men. The healing of the paralytic showed the people that men's sins could be forgiven; it also demonstrated God's presence among them in the person of Jesus Christ.

Jesus offered the kingdom to all on the condition of repentance from their sin to the tax collector, to the woman of Samaria at the well, and to Mary Magdalene who was caught in adultery. Most of all, He offers the kingdom of Salvation of eternal life to all people today on the same condition: repent from your sins and pray for forgiveness, which is only through Jesus Christ.

Jesus taught that God would forgive the repentant heart; Jesus actively sought out the sinners and offered them the possibility of forgiveness. Forgiveness occurs when we see our sin as God sees it, because, when we sin against each other, we sin against God.

When we ask for forgiveness of our sins from God, we must forgive others who knowingly and unknowingly hurt us. The Holy Spirit empowers believers to know the right way to forgive those who do wrong things against them.

We have to lead an important way of life in order to forgive others. Forgiving others is difficult, but Christ wants believers to make it an important aspect of Christian life.

## The Spirit Power

If we faithfully and truly want to live in a good relationship with God, we have to learn or pray that the Holy Spirit enlightens our heart to the Spirit of forgiveness for others. The main reason is that we want to be like Jesus. Here are more verses that shed light on the fruit of forgiveness: Matt. 18:23-35, Col. 3:12-15, Eph. 1:7, and 1 John 1:7-9.

# 8

# Forbearance

Forbearance is a great Christian duty. However, indifferent to the distinction between truth and error is not thereby encouraged. The strong must bear the weak.

"We then that are strong ought to bear the infirmities of the weak, and not to please ourselves. Let every one of us please his neighbor for his good to edification." Rom. 15: 1-2.

Another meaning of forbearance is refraining from anger or provocation when someone offends us, and controlling ourselves and showing patience in these circumstances or situations.

"Or despisest thou the riches of his goodness and forbearance and longsuffering; not knowing that the goodness of God leadeth thee to repentance?" Rom. 2:4.

"Whom God hath set forth to be a propitiation through faith in his blood, to declare his righteousness for the remission of sins that are past, through the forbearance of God." Rom. 3:25. Christ was the sacrifice and offering.

Christ suffered death as the consequence for our sin; it was propitiatory, that Christ's death for the sinners satisfied God's righteous nature and His moral order, thereby removing his wrath from repentant sinners. In accordance with God's integrity, sin must be punished and propitiation made for sinners.

We have learned that the judgment of God sometimes delayed. This is the evidence of His dealing with sinners or evildoers and His own forbearance in holding back punishment on the wicked and rebellious.

God continues to exercise His self-restraint in spite of man's ceaseless provocation. God's providence, protection, preservation, and love continue to lead men and women into repentance. He does not want anyone to perish, but rather, to come to the knowledge of repentance.

Christ's death for sinners satisfied God's righteous nature and His moral order, thereby removing His wrath against repentant sinners. It was a victory on the cross as Christ fought and triumphed over the power of sin.

Christ's death was the initial, or first, victory over the spiritual enemies of both God and humanity. Christ died for the sake of others; thus, the redemptive work of Christ was complete. God received the glory.

Forbearance refers to God's patience as expressed through His willingness to hold back for a time, God's forbearance does not mean that God allows sin, but that he gives sinners many, many opportunities to change and repent from their sins.

God is a righteous judge over the past, present, and future sins of the children of Israel and of those who are believers in Jesus Christ. God's forbearance gave the Jews and Gentiles the blessing of salvation and eternal life.

# 9

# Truth

Truth is what you know it to be. The truth is always known to those who will seek it. God is true. He is God; there is no other. God is faithful and in all His ways, He is a compassionate and gracious God.

God is the God of truth. He truthfully revealed Himself to the people of Israel and to all people in the world. God's ways and purposes are incomprehensible and beyond finding out. God came to earth in the person of His Son, Jesus Christ, to save the world and redeem us from our past, present, and future sins.

He revealed His true existence through our Lord and Savior Jesus Christ. The Book of Hebrews says, "God, who at sundry times and in divers manners spake in time past unto the fathers by the prophets, hath in these last days spoken unto us by his Son, whom he hath appointed heir of all things, by whom also he made the worlds." Heb. 1:1-2.

The True God has come to live among us and gave us His divine plan through Jesus Christ His Son. "For God so loved the world, that he gave his only begotten Son, that whosoever believeth in him should not perish, but have everlasting life." John 3:16.

God gave His Son on the cross as an offering for the sins of humanity. Christ's atonement proceeds from the loving heart of God. The Son willingly offered Himself for our sins. Christ is our sin bearer. "Jesus saith unto him I am the way, the truth, and the life: no man cometh unto the Father, but by me."

John 14:6. The Lord Jesus Christ made clear, then and now, that He is the only way to heaven. Christ is not one of many ways to heaven He is the only way. Jesus made clear that He is truth, the embodiment of the truth. All believers in Christ abide in the truth of Christ. Jesus Christ our Lord is life, the source of life, the beginning of life, and the end of life.

All believers in Christ automatically received the life of Christ immediately after conversion. They also receive the gift of eternal because He is life. Jesus said the people of this world, including believers, shall know the truth and the truth shall set you free.

"Howbeit when he, the Spirit of truth, is come, he will guide you into all truth: for he shall not speak of himself; but whatsoever he shall hear, that shall he speak: and he will shew you things to come." John 16:13.

The work of the Holy Spirit is not only directed to the unsaved; it is also indicated that the power of the Spirit operates on all believers and in the Church in order to teach, correct, and guide them all to truth.

Christ's preaching helps believers follow the commandments of God and worship Him in the Spirit of Holiness. The Holy Spirit helps us to know the truth of everything that is going on in our world, through the authority of the Word of God.

Believers must stay in the Word of God so that the Spirit of God may continue to produce the Spirit of truth within them and also flow to other people, helping them to know the truth, live truthful lives, follow the truth, and manifest the truth of God in every circumstance and in all the areas of their lives.

When believers in Christ maintain good relationships with God, they walk in the Spirit and live by the truth of God's Word; they also produce good works that are pleasing to Him because Christ's Spirit rules in their hearts through the operation of the Holy Spirit.

God, through His Spirit, directs and controls believers' lives, moment-by-moment, everyday; when this happens, it means we become alive in God in order to do God's will. It is very difficult for some believers to live a life of the truth of God.

Some believers think they have the Spirit, but they don't because they have not fully surrendered to the Spirit's control of their lives. Walk in the Spirit, live holy lives, listen to the words of God, and obey His commands concerning His will for our lives.

We must be able to do good work that pleases Him. Believers who fall into sin must confess their sins and be restored through the power of the Holy Spirit.

# 10

# Temperance

Temperance is similar to self-control. Temperance or self-control depends upon the believer's objectivity in establishing boundaries for his or her demeanor, actions, thoughts, emotions, processes, decision-making work, will, and desires that may trouble or be graven in his or her mind.

Temperate believers will avoid anything that will take them to extremes that they will not be able to control, such as personal behaviors, bad habits, expression of negative opinions in words, actions, or deeds.

Believers with the fruit of temperance have and maintain control over their willpower, which is the strength of the mind to make strong decisions and plans, and to carry out God's Master plan according to His will, that has been called the blueprint of our lives.

Believers read the Word of God, daily, in order to be strong in their decision making or other things for which believers need to exercise willpower. "All things are lawful unto me, but all things are not expedient: all things are lawful for me, but I will not be brought under the power of any." 1 Cor. 6:12.

All believers must be able to exercise the fruit of the Spirit temperance over everything that they do, either in their homes or in public.

If our actions do not conform to the Word of God, we must refrain from such practices or behaviors. Believers must apply Spiritual discipline in certain areas of their lives.

Believers must be able to promote the quality of good character. As the Holy Spirit pours His power and produces His fruits within us, we must be careful what we say. When we are growing in the knowledge of the Word of God with the supernatural powers of using these spiritual gifts, we must especially exercise temperance to control and guide us, and we must be fully subjected to the control of the Holy Spirit.

"Whoso keepeth his mouth and his tongue keepeth his soul from troubles." Prov. 21:23. All believers are encouraged to watch their tongues. The tongue is so powerful that it can destroy relationships, friendships, and even cause death unexpectedly it can set the whole body on fire.

"The tongue of the wise useth knowledge aright: but the mouth of fools poureth out foolishness." Prov. 15:2.

All believers should give gentle answers to questions when others are angry to encourage peace that will show the fruit of the Spirit in them. Believers who want to live lives marked by a full relationship with Christ, must crucify themselves and establish boundaries for a lives of temperance under the control of the Spirit of God.

Believers in the Lord Jesus Christ must produce the fruits of the Spirit of temperance and self-control in order to be able to focus on well determined behavior that will help them to reach the goals set before them by the Lord.

A lack of temperance in the lives of some believers makes it difficult for them to turn their lives around and completely in order to follow Christ. A lack of self-control and temperance has changed believers' vision of life in God's Spirit.

The Holy Spirit produces temperance in all believers so that they may remain steadfast in the right direction that will help them to achieve their goals and dreams. "But I keep under my body, and bring it into subjection: lest that by any means, when I have preached to others, I myself should be a castaway." 1 Cor. 9:27.

Christian life requires self-control, temperance, and self-discipline we must practice and make them a permanent way of living. All Christians must learn how to control themselves and abide with the Spirit's control of temperance, denying human nature and its compulsions to satisfy desires.

Sacrificing ourselves is necessary if we are to stop sinning as a way of life. We must practice temperance self-denial, and self-sacrifice. With an understanding of self-control, we will be able to see our need for temperance in our lives more clearly.

Believers must not limit their understanding to individual passions and appetites, but rather, maintain good sense, sober minds, wisdom, moderation, and good, sound minds. We must keep our lives under the Spirit's control to produce all that we need for life and godliness.

# 11

# Humbleness

Humbleness or humility is the opposite of anyone who thinks that he is better than someone else, exercising the Spirit of pride. "Likewise, ye younger, submit yourselves unto the elder.

"Yea, all of you be subject one to another, and be cloth with humility: for God resisteth the proud, and giveth grace to the humble.

"Humble yourselves therefore under the mighty hand of God, that he may exalt you in due time." 1 Pet. 5:5-6.

Humility should be the symbol of all Christians; there should be no sign of pride in Christian character. Pride brings contention, shame, and destruction upon the people who exercise it. "And being found in fashion as a man, he humbled himself, and became obedient unto death, even the death of the cross." Php. 2:8.

Apostle Paul told us that Christ left His Father's glory in heaven and took the humble position of a servant, made Himself nothing, emptied himself of everything but love, and endured the shameful, painful cross for us sinners we should follow His footsteps. Love and truth lead to humility. God loves all of us equally.

Believers should praise and encourage the people around them with the Spirit of humility; other people will also humble themselves in return. Jesus said, "And said unto them, whosoever shall receive this child in my name receiveth me: and whosoever shall receiveth me receiveth him that sent me: for He that is least among you all, the same shall be great." Luke 9:48.

Our Lord was teaching about and referring to the believers who will humble themselves in the cause of following Him; He told them that humility is the key. "Humble yourselves in the sight of the Lord and He shall lift you up." Jas. 4:10.

God gives believers who humbly submit and draw near to Him abundant grace and mercy to help them in all troubles and adversities in life. Humility stands as one of the foundational teachings for having and growing a fruitful Christian life.

Humility holds the secret for growth, wisdom, perseverance, blessings, salvation, and wonderful relationships. Jesus wants all Christians to be humble believers to humble themselves with the help of God.

Christ's obedience and humbleness were evident on the cross. If we allow the Holy Spirit to move through us we will be able to humble ourselves through the power of the Lord. When we allow the Lord Jesus Christ to come into our hearts as our Savior, we receive salvation and eternal life.

Believers must give the lordship of their lives to Jesus Christ. Studying the Word of God is also very important in the lives of believers. It helps them build godly wisdom and understand the world around them.

Humbleness helps us increase our faith in the Lord and follow Jesus all the days of our lives. It takes a humble Spirit before the Lord to truly know the mind and the heart of God. Christ is the Good Shepherd.

We believers must follow wherever He leads. Believers must humble themselves and submit to the Holy Spirit, who will lead them to the Lord. This is the foundation of all aspects of humility.

The Holy Spirit produced the fruit of humility in us; the sign of the Holy Spirit begins by giving God first place in our hearts, decision making, actions, attitude, motivations, and repentance of sin. We demonstrate pride when we are unable or unwilling to correct wrongs and injustices in our lives and in other people's lives.

Humble believers will not boast of who they are or what they are doing or going to do. "But he that is greatest among you shall be your servant." Matt. 23:11.

Humility is found in the way that we think of ourselves and others. A humble believer in Jesus will think of God and others first, before thinking about himself. All Christians must be humble and be servants to others.

A humble person is someone who acknowledges his or her place, like John the Baptist who cried out: "And preached, saying, there cometh one mightier than I after me, the latchet of whose shoes I am not worthy to stoop down and unloose." Mark 1:7.

John the Baptist was the first person who preached the good news concerning Christ. He was sent ahead of Jesus to prepare the way for the revelation of God in His incarnate Son Jesus Christ.

Believers must be like Christ and humble themselves; this is done by becoming servants to others with the use of our abilities, not by denying our abilities. We must give honor to others, not to ourselves.

"And lest I should be exalted above measure through the abundance of the revelations, there was given to me a thorn in the flesh, the messenger of Satan to buffet me, lest I should be exalted above measure." 2 Cor. 12:7.

The word "thorn" stands for pain, suffering, and humiliation, but it does not lead to sin. Paul's thorn was given to keep him from becoming proud about the revelations that he had received. Paul's thorn kept him to close to God.

Sometimes, in order to fulfill His promise in our lives, God can develop a program of humility in us, subjecting us to humiliating circumstances or otherwise providing sources of humiliation in our life. This type of God's activities in our lives is good for our spiritual maturity; it helps us to develop and maintain humility.

This is essential in Christian characters. Whereas a proud person may not recognize pride in themselves, those who are not subject to humiliation tend to develop pride. One source of humiliation for someone might be another person's pride.

# 12

# Self-Esteem

Self-esteem contains three views for every individual human being—the view of God that the Holy Spirit has for us.

The opinions that others hold concerning us constitute the way other people view us and see us. The perception that we have of ourselves constitutes the way we see ourselves and value ourselves. God looks at the heart of every human being.

"And needed not that any should testify of man: for He knew what was in man." John 2:25. There are certain ways in which self-perception may become inflated. We, as believers in Jesus, must be careful not to think more highly about ourselves than we ought to think.

Believers must not be high minded; we must have a good and healthy view of ourselves. Jesus commands or instructs that we should love our neighbors as we love ourselves.

Many people have self-esteem related to how they perceive themselves physically. Their character may make an initial impression upon others. Knowledge of God's Word is the best fruit of the Spirit for all believers of Christ to exhibit.

Physical or emotional abuse may cause low self-esteem and the Spirit of God will bless that believer with strength to overcome all past injuries, physically, emotionally, or spiritually. These types of low self-esteem usually occur during early childhood.

Low self-esteem is an attitude that dwells within the individual, which usually is reflected in the behavior of the person. Christ's teaching reveals that, "For from within, out of the heart of men, proceed evil thoughts, adulteries, fornications, murders." Mark 7:21.

An impure heart will corrupt one's thoughts, feelings, words, and actions, while a heart that is full of the Spirit of God will live a life in Christ. An individual who holds an unhealthy view of himself manifests this view in many areas and in many distressing ways.

Thousands of neglected children suffer from low self-esteem because of broken homes or the drug abuse of a parent; children in foster care suffer from low self-esteem because they have no parents or anyone around to give them love and affection.

The Word of God teaches us that we must be aware of the life God has created for us. We must always be careful with our dignity and our depravity two extreme character traits that may appear in our lives. We must not try to change from one direction to the other, or go too far from one direction to another;. This will remove us completely from the path that the power of the Holy Spirit has set before us.

When we tend to rely on dignity, we become arrogant and sin can creep in through the open door of arrogance. Those who have low self-esteem tend to dislike themselves for unnecessary reasons. God, who knows the human heart, has provided the cure.

Jesus Christ God the Son came to earth in our own form and paid for our sins on the cross; on the cross our salvation was completed. We were bought by the precious blood of Jesus Christ, our Redeemer.

Believers should understand that we have been chosen and redeemed through Christ's life; we have gained value that is beyond compare. Knowing that we are worthless, we humble ourselves before God, which allows us to value and be grateful for God's grace and love, given to us even though we do not deserve it.

Through grace, He gave us the blessing of eternal life. God loves us and the blood of the Lamb redeems us. Your true worth or value is not measured by your financial statements or job title; you are precious because you are a creation of the highest order of intelligence.

True self-esteem is not something you control by yourself; it is something that you can gain through a real relationship with God. Happiness, joyful life, and feeling good about oneself, come not through acquiring things, but by contributing things.

Self-confidence comes from accepting one's imperfections, limitations, and the things we cannot change. Low self-esteem is a feeling of worthlessness or having an inferiority complex about oneself.

True humility acknowledges that human beings are finite creations of God to whom He has given new lives. He made us new creations through our Lord and Savior and continues to bless us with abilities to use for living for Him and serving Him forever and for being able to serve others.

There are two extremes in the Christian community. One involves those who think too highly of themselves, which we call spiritual arrogance. Self-esteem is the view one holds about himself or herself and how someone values, judges, or sees himself or herself on a scale of one to ten.

"Wherefore I give you to understand, that no man speaking by the Spirit of God calleth Jesus accursed: and that no man can say that Jesus is the Lord, but by the Holy Ghost." Rom. 12:3.

There are also those who suffer from spiritual inferiority, seeing themselves as worthless in the kingdom of God. Jesus took a humble position when He washed the disciples' feet. "Now before the feast of the Passover, when Jesus knew that his hour was come that he should depart out of this world unto the Father, having loved his own which were in the world, he loved them unto the end." John 13:1.

Paul advised all believers to be humble in exercising their spiritual gifts. We should know that each one of us is unique and that we all have an important assignment to perform for our Lord and Savior.

There is a great deal of spiritual arrogance that it is difficult to correct in the Church; sometimes even the most mature Christians struggle with arrogance and become so proud that they become no longer teachable. For example, this can happen if we begin to feel self-sufficient and trust in ourselves instead of trusting God.

Sometimes, this can make the whole Church become competitive and everyone can become secluded in their own cycles, instead of coming together as one family of God. "Take my yoke upon you, and learn of me; for I am meek and lowly in heart: and ye shall find rest unto your souls." Matt. 11:29.

This is the rest that we find and experience by serving Jesus Christ. If you come, follow Christ, become His servant, and obey His control, He will give you rest in your soul, a blessing of peace, and the gift of the Holy Spirit to lead you throughout your life.

Many people become arrogant because of their position of leadership in the Church or their friendship with highly political people. Other people are more proud because of their spiritual gifts and experiences, for example, speaking in tongues.

They feel that they are more spiritual in the church and more powerful than others in the church. This constitutes the spiritual arrogance of unaware believers in the church.

# 13

# Righteousness

Righteousness means uprightness. Righteousness is the fulfillment of the terms of a covenant between God and humanity or between humans in the full range of human relationships.

God's righteousness is what God does in fulfillment of the terms of the covenant that God established with His chosen people of Israel. "But who is able to build him a house, seeing the heaven and heaven of heavens cannot contain him? Who am I then, that I should build him an house, save only to born sacrifice before him?" 2 Chron. 12:6.

"Oh let the wickedness of the wicked come to an end; but establish the just: for the righteous God trieth the hearts of reins." Psl. 7:9.

God's righteousness is a divine experience for those within the covenant community. God's righteousness was understood as the judgment, protection, and deliverance of Israel from their enemies. Salvation and condemnation are also part of God's righteousness.

The Holy Spirit teaches that the righteous can expect God to deliver and help them in. God's righteousness, based on believers' salvation, is the pure work of God. God's saving activity maintains the divine side of the covenant of creation.

God's action in Christ created faith on the part of human beings through the power of the Holy Spirit. Therefore, God's righteousness is the power of God's work for saving the faith of humanity and all creation, through the creation of faith in sinful people.

God's righteousness means God gives the possibility of righteous salvation to humans. Righteousness is something that God requires from humanity, especially all Christians, and which God gives as a gift to people of faith. We can say that faith is the condition for the gift of righteousness.

God gave righteousness in recognition of and for faith in Jesus Christ. Therefore, God's righteousness is the tool and key for understanding the salvation of people. Righteousness is proof that a person or believer in Christ is living a life that is pleasing in His sight. God's righteousness is the natural expression of His holiness.

God is always right. God is a righteous God there is no unrighteousness in Him. God is always consistent without partiality. God's actions are always right and true. "Blessed are they which do hunger and thirst after righteousness: for they shall be filled." Matt. 5:6.

Our Lord made it clear that the fundamental requirement for Godly living is to thirst and hunger for righteousness; an example of this is that of Moses in the wilderness with the people of Israel.

The spiritual state of all believers throughout their lives should depend on their thirst for the presence of God and for close communion and fellowship with Christ and the Holy Spirit. "But seek ye first the kingdom of God, and his righteousness; and all these things shall be added unto you." Matt. 6:33.

All believers are advised to seek God's kingdom and His righteousness, we must continuously and sincerely search, look for, and seek to have the power of God demonstrated, displayed, and assembled in our lives.

We pray that God's kingdom come, with the mighty power of the Holy Spirit for the saving of sinners and deliverance of His people from the bondage of evil and wicked people. "For with the man believeth unto righteousness; and with the mouth confession is made unto salvation." Rom. 10:10.

At the center of belief in the lordship of Jesus Christ and his death, burial, and resurrection is righteousness. Believers must believe the truth about Jesus with all their minds and respond in their hearts with commitment to Christ, in their words and deeds.

God the Father is righteous; Jesus Christ the Son of God is righteous.

The Father, through the Son and in the Spirit, gives the gift of righteousness to repentant sinners for salvation. Believing sinners are declared righteous by the Father, through the Son, and made righteous by the Holy Spirit working in them, and they will be wholly righteous in the ages to come.

Believers in Jesus Christ are called to live righteously within the sight of God, which means living according to God's will.

All believers are within the covenantal relationship with God's gift of salvation; they are to behave as the people of the Holy God. "Sow to yourselves in righteousness, reap in mercy; break up your fallow ground: for it is time to seek the Lord, till He come and rain righteousness upon you." Hos. 10:12.

The people of Hosea's time needed to break their hearts and minds, because of the sorrow of their sin, and to repent, which would open them to the word and of God. They continued to earnestly seek God, until they were again restored and experienced His love and mercy. John the Baptist called for repentance and righteous behavior such as is pleasing to God.

"Bring forth therefore fruits worthy of repentance, and begin not to say within yourselves, we have Abraham to our father: for I say unto you, that God is able of these stones to raise up children unto Abraham."

Luke 3:8. Believers must know that genuine repentance will bring the fruit of righteousness.

True saving faith and conversion to Jesus Christ is clearly evident in lives that have forsaken sin and that bear godly fruit. Those who say that they believe in Christ Jesus and that they are children of God, but do not live lives that produce good fruit, are like trees that will be cut down and thrown into the fire.

It was on the basis of that righteousness that John the Baptist baptized Jesus in the River Jordan. Jesus also, in His teaching, presented righteousness in one's whole life, inward and outward, as seen by God, as the requirement for entrance into the kingdom of heaven.

Christ told the Scribes and Pharisees that He was the Messiah the fulfillment of the law and the prophet. From the Gospel of Matthew to the Gospel of John, all four Gospels made it clear that, from the beginning, Jesus' mission has been to fulfill God's righteousness.

"That whosoever believeth in him should not perish, but have eternal life." John 3:15. It was made clear that the kingdom, ministry, and salvation were, in His words, in Him and had come through Him.

Righteousness of a new covenant is brought about by correct thinking, feeling, speaking, and behavior on the part of believers who are required to enter into the kingdom that God approves and commands.

The Holy Spirit *Paraclete* has a specific role with respect to righteousness. "And when he is come, he will reprove the world of sin, and of righteousness, and of judgment." John 16:8. The work of the Holy Spirit in the world, through Jesus Christ the Messiah, is to convince the world of righteousness.

The Spirit vindicated Jesus as the righteous one, when the Father raised Him from the dead and exalted Him at His right hand in heaven. The righteousness of God, provided by the grace of God, was provided for everyone who believes. God is called Jehovah, "Tsidkenu," and The Lord our Righteousness.

God's righteousness is revealed through His prophets in the Old Testament. His commandments to the people of Israel and through His Son Jesus Christ and the Bible also provided human beings with His righteousness being human.

Christ's death and resurrection also revealed that righteousness can only come from, and through, Jesus Christ. God is the source of all good things in the world, since before the beginning of creation. He is right and just and full of love.

There is no unrighteousness in Him. God sends His Holy Spirit into the hearts of believers so that they can pray, get close to Him, and worship Him. The Christian point of view is that righteousness is being in upright standing, good standing, with God because of Christ's death on the cross and His resurrection.

A person can be righteous if he or she possesses God's character, because all righteousness comes from the Spirit of God who produces the fruit of righteousness in the lives of all believers of Jesus Christ. The Spirit of God helps believers to live righteous lives in Him.

# 14

# Meekness

Many people do not know what meekness is all about. A lot of people believe that when someone is meek, means the person is weak; but in reality, meekness is not a sign of weakness.

Meek people are always very strong. They always like to help other people around them. Meek people deal with others, whether believers or non-believers, with the Spirit of goodness.

They accept the will of God for their lives without hesitation or resistance, and they don't react or complain when others are given priority over them.

They endure and patiently exercise patience and longsuffering when they are being treated unjustly. Meek people do not seek revenge or retaliate when someone hurts them.

A meek believer is one who exercises strength; He or she is always in control, without looking for a reward. Our Lord Jesus was a meek person on earth, with His strength under control. Moses was a meek person during journey in the wilderness of the children of Israel.

Meekness is a condition of a believer's heart and mind, while gentleness describes a believer's actions. Meekness finds its strength from longsuffering and patience, while patience expresses itself through love.

A meek believer is very mild and patient, and has a teachable Spirit. They always believe in God and heaven, "Blessed be the God and Father of our Lord Jesus Christ, who hath blessed us withal spiritual blessings in heavenly places in Christ." Eph. 1:3.

Meek people always leave every circumstance that they are going through in the hands of God. "To speak evil of no man, to be no brawlers, but gentle, shewing all meekness unto all men." Titus 3:2.

Meek believers have a passion for serving God and others; meek people are so mild, that there is no temper or bitterness in them. God always rewards the meek. "Blessed are the meek: for they shall inherit the earth." Matt. 5:5.

"When God arose to judgment, to save all the meek of the earth." Psl. 76:9. "For the Lord taketh pleasure in his people He will beautify the meek with salvation." Psl. 149:4.

"Now I Paul myself beseech you by the meekness and gentleness of Christ, who in presence am base among you, but absent am bold toward you." 2 Cor. 10:1.

"Now the man Moses was very meek, above all the men which were upon the face of the earth." Num. 12:3. Moses' humility relied on his trust in God; he was free of selfishness and ungodly characters. Moses depended on God and trusted Him for help and as his defender throughout his service to the Lord, to the point that God was delighted to help him whenever he called on God.

Meekness combined with humility before God is of great value. In spreading God's Word: "But sanctify the Lord God in your hearts: and be ready always to give an answer to every man that asked you a reason of the hope that is in you with meekness and fear." 1 Pet. 3:15.

"Wherefore lay apart all filthiness and superfluity of naughtiness, and receive with meekness the engrafted word, which is able to save your souls." Jas. 1:21. Meekness goes with humility in dealing with men, winning sinners back to God, and trespassing.

"Brethren, if a man be overtaken in a fault, ye which are spiritual, restore such a one in the Spirit of meekness; considering thyself, lest thou also be tempted." Gal. 6:1. Believers should be restored back to true repentance and to full commitment with the Lord Jesus Christ and His ways.

Believers must exercise the Spirit of perseverance, which is one of the required qualifications for serving Christ. Meekness is a fruit of the Spirit. Many people associate meekness with weakness and timidity. The Bible says that Moses was very meek, more so than all men who were upon the face of the earth.

Meekness is an attribute of God Almighty Himself, and it is very important to know that we were made in the image of God and that we are His true witnesses. It is a characteristic of a life of contentment.

Our Lord mentioned meekness in His teaching of the Sermon on the Mount, "Blessed are the meek: for they shall inherit the earth." Matt. 5:5. This means that the meek will share in the earth's inheritance.

Moses was one of the greatest of God's servants. He gently and mildly served God with a spirit of submission. Nevertheless, we have to know that the Spirit of God was the one who produced the fruit of the Spirit of meekness in Moses, throughout his service to God on earth.

The Holy Spirit manifests the fruit of meekness in all those who belong to Christ; it's the Spirit Power that helps all believers to endure pain or hurt, with patience and without resentment.

Because the Spirit of God will not dwell in heart that are full of resentment, God command all believers to be indwelt with the Spirit of meekness. He empowers His children with the Spirit of meekness so that they may bear more and more fruit into His kingdom.

God always rewards those who are meek among us those who practice and exercise the fruits of meekness and gentleness. Meekness is both internal and external, and should be present in all of our activities in our lives.

Many believers need the fruit of meekness in order to serve our Lord and Savior, especially in the missionary field. For example, meekness is needed when a believer tries to correct, restore, or advise in the Church, or when a believer is witnessing or trying to defend the Gospel to those who are non-believers or haters of God, correcting their opponents with the truth of the Gospel message.

Meekness is the fruit of the Spirit by which the Holy Spirit produces learning tools for aligning Christian lives and also for living disciplined lives.

A meek character always stands for the truth, as well as for the correction of any false religion. The main idea of meekness is not based on our relationships with others or on who we are, but rather, it is based on our inward development of tenderheartedness.

It is the attitude with which we accept God's will and finality in our lives, without resisting or disputing. When we do this, we are exercising the fruit of meekness. When meekness endures with patience and gentleness, it creates a soft manner through which the power of the Spirit of God passes.

In order to have the Spirit of meekness we must be born again in Christ. The life of Moses shows that meekness is not weakness, but strength under

## The Spirit Power

control. The more we understand and develop the Spirit of meekness, the more we take on the nature of our Lord and Savior.

Therefore, it is understandable that Jesus taught discipleship by praising and acknowledging the quality of meekness. The goal of Paul the Apostle was to know Christ and the power of his resurrection. "That I may know him, and the power of his resurrection, and the fellowship of his sufferings, being made conformable unto his death." Php. 3:10.

Apostle Paul's goal, which should also be the goal of all believer was to know Christ intimately as a person and to follow His ways, nature, and character, as revealed in the Word of God.

God's Salvation is available to everyone, but only the meek can understand and respond to it. It is the power of the Holy Spirit's transforming power. The outpouring of the Spirit fruit of meekness enables believers to make God's Word part of their minds, wills, and emotions are and to forget their sinful habits.

Meek believers make right decisions when they really turn to the Lord with the spirit of meekness and demonstrate the qualities of the fruit of meekness. The Lord Jesus Christ will direct all of the decisions that we are making or about to make. Jesus Christ is the same yesterday, today, and forever. He has the power to direct our decisions with the Spirit Power.

Meekness has to do with steadfastness in our serving the Lord. It is the power of the Holy Spirit that is always under control, not out of control; it applies to believers who are strong and strengthened in Christ with the whole armor of God. "But thou, O man of God flee these things; and follow after righteousness, godliness, faith, love, patience, meekness." 1 Tim. 6:10.

In the Old Testament, prophets were called men of God. The same thing happened when Apostle Paul called Timothy a man of God. A man of God demonstrates the love of God that the Holy Spirit plants in him; believers must make other people around them think about, see, and glorify God within them.

All believers must flee from lives of impurity, discontent, and foolish and harmful lusts. Christians should cultivate their character a clean character of righteousness which speaks of justice and integrity in dealing with other people.

# Summary

Complete, full knowledge of and inspiration from the entire Bible is equally God-given from Genesis through Revelation.

The Word of God, through Biblical inerrancy, points to the doctrinal position that the Bible is accurate and totally free of error, that Scripture in its original manuscripts does not affirm anything that is not true not only with regards to doctrine, but also with regards to history, science, chronology, and in all other areas of life.

The doctrine of the Trinity is considered as being at the center of Christian doctrine. God reveals Himself to humanity through so many of the things that He has created, in such a way that all of His creations may find their meaning in relation to God.

The Spirit Power assists all Christians, including students and scholars of theology, who are interested in understanding their Christians life, in their hearts and minds.

This book will be a great resource and a treasure. This book will help all Christians and theology students of all denominations, as well as all people of the other religions, to open up the Scripture for a greater spiritual understanding of the Spirit Power and open them to the things of God, His power, and His will for all people on earth.

The Power of the Holy Spirit in the lives of all believers in the body of Christ on this earth cannot be compared to any power. It is incomparable, it is immeasurable and incomprehensible beyond what anyone can think or imagine.

Our Lord said, "But the hour cometh, and now is, when the true worshippers shall worship the Father in Spirit and in truth: for the Father seeketh such to worship Him." John 4:23.

Jesus Christ expounded upon this clearly to the Samaritan woman at the well. We must come to God with sincere hearts and with the Spirit of holiness, leading lives that are under the control of the Holy Spirit because we are created in the image of God.

Our new birth is different from our old birth, which was of the flesh. God's relationship with all of His children is based on the Spirit not on the flesh. It is like the relationship of a Father and His children it can never be erased.

We are one in Him as He is one with the Father. We must worship the Father according to the truth of the Father that was revealed by the Son and that the Holy Spirit controls and guides. The relationship that God requires of us must be a voluntary one that we enter into willingly and joyfully, surrendering our will to the will of God.

Our relationship must remain unconditional and be based on our faith in Christ, throughout our life on earth. Faith demonstrates and is characterized by sincere love and obedience to God.

The only true worship is when we worship the Father through the Spirit of Holiness. God gave us His Spirit and He continues to pour out His Spirit on all those who believe in Him, up until today.

Every day, there is always a day of Pentecost in heaven, whereby the Spirit of God pours down into the hearts, minds, and souls of His converted sinners. God gave us the power of the Spirit to dwell and perform

His supernatural power through us, so that we may be able to live lives originating in the Lord here on earth. I urge all members of the body of Christ to claim this power, and use it everywhere, in everything we do; He is waiting for you and me.

There is no power but the power of the Spirit of God in our lives, in the lives of our children, relatives and friends. Use the power of the Spirit of God in your office, neighborhood, community, city, state, and in the entire world with the unending love of the Spirit that dwells in you.

## The Spirit Power

Exercise all the fruit of the Spirit wherever you go: love, joy, peace, goodness, kindness, and the other fruits of the Spirit. Allow the Spirit of God to continuously produce and pour out the fruits of His Spirit onto our lives.

The Spirit of God the Father, the Spirit of God the Son, and the Spirit of God the Holy Spirit is one, and He made us one in Him. We should rejoice and continue in unending love and in the Spirit Power. Jesus Christ is the truth; all believers must live in unity and speak the truth that Christ requires of us.

Those who do not have the truth in them hide what is in their hearts and they, remain in darkness and automatically throw themselves outside the kingdom of heaven. Believers must speak the truth with the love of God.

# Bibliography

Walter A. Walter Editor Evangelical Dictionary of Biblical Dictionary of Biblical Theology: Publisher Baker Book House, Grand Rapids, MI, USA.

William MacDonald, Edited by Art Farstad: Believer's Bible Commentary, Thomas Nelson Publisher, Nashville, TN, USA.

Thomas F. Torrance, Paul D. Molnar 1946. Ashgate publisher, Ltd: Distributed by Syndetic Solutions, Inc. Theologian of the Trinity. Christian Denominations Doctrine Theology the Bible. Farnham, England, Burlington, VT, USA.

Mathew Henry's Commentary in one Volume, Edited by Re. Leslie F. Church: Zondervan Publishing House, Grand Rapids, MI, USA.

D. Norman Geisler: Systematic Theology Volume Four, Church Last Thing, Bethany House Publishers, Bloomington, MN, USA.

Leadership Ministries Worldwide: Practical Word Studies in the New Testament Volume One and Volume Two from the Publishers of The Preacher's Outline and Sermon Bible: Zondervan Publishing House, Chattanooga, TN, USA.

James D. Smart: The Interpretation of Scripture, the Westminster Press, Philadelphia, PA, USA.

# Biblical Index

Genesis: 1:2, 6:3, 41:38, 2:7, 2:9, 15:6, 2:16, 22, 1:19

Exodus: 31:3, 35:31, 14:22, 13:14, 32:23, 34:6

Leviticus: 19:2

Numbers: 12:3, 11-13, 11:17, 6:24-26, 14:18

Deuteronomy: 34:9, 6:4, 7:9

Joshua 1:9, 3:15-16

2 Samuel: 9:1-13

2 Kings: 2:2

2 Chronicles: 2:6

Nehemiah: 8:10, 12:43

Job: 33:4, 20:4-5

Psalms: 23:6, 57:11, 76:9, 149:4, 34:8, 104:30, 119:11, 139:7, 51:6-10, 3:5,16:11, 81:1,16, 16:11, 30:5, 5:11-12, 37:7, 140:1, 46:10, 103:8, 145:8-9, 86:15, 51:1, 34:8, 25:9

Proverbs: 14:13, 9:10, 45:6-7, 15:21, 14:29, 15:18, 19:11, 3:5-6, 19:22, 51:1, 11:17, 15:1, 28:20, 21:23, 15:2

Ecclesiastes: 2:1-11, 26
Isaiah: 4:4, 55:8-9, 65:3, 42:1, 26:3, 30:18, 25:1, 53:7-9
Jeremiah: 15:15, 29::11, 17:7-8
Ezekiel: 36:26-27, 37:3-5
Hosea: 10:12, 2:20
Joel: 2:13, 2:28-32
Zechariah: 4:6
Matthew: 28:19-20, 5:1-12, 25:21, 9:17, 19:17, 11:23-24, 6:4, 6, 11:29, 5:5-6, 9:3-6, 18:23-35, 8:4, 9:3-6, 18:23-35 8:4, 5:6, 6:33 11:11
Mark: 16:16
Luke: 23:34, 1:35, 2:10-11, 13:34, 6:35-36, 6:45, 11:13, 7:47, 22:4, 6:45, 16:10-12, 18:7, 9:48, 9:48, 3:8, 19:23
John: 4:24, 1:3, 1:1, 4:23-24, 14:7-9, 15:1-2, 14:16, 26, 16:8, 16:13, 16:7-8, 3:6, 6:63, 4:14, 7:37-38, 3:3-8, 86:16, 4:23-24, 15:10, 13:35, 4:7-8, 3:16, 15:13, 4:19, 1:11, 6:44, 17:13, 15:11, 14:27, 12:27, 16:13, 13:17, 1:7-9, 20:24-31, 3:3, 20:26, 16:22, 20:21, 16, 12-14, 20:21, 16:21, 4:23, 14:6, 16:13, 6:12, 2:25, 13:1
Acts: 11:16-17, 2:3-4, 2:38, 8:14-15, 3:31, 24:24-25, 9:17, 10:44, 1:8, 1:4, 5:31, 16:30, 12:46, 16:34, 16:24-25, 10:36, 8:35-38
Romans: 8:16, 8:16-17, 6:3-4, 8:15-16, 8:27, 1:29-31, 13:13, 5:5, 8:14, 16:20, 8:25, 2:4, 11:22, 5:8, 8:11, 5:1, 15:13, 12:21, 10:17, 7:14-17, 8:3-4, 2:4, 9:22-24, 15:1-2, 10:10, 2:4, 3:25, 12:3

## The Spirit Power

1 Corinthians: 10:31, 6:6-10, 13:1-13, 8:1, 13:4-8, 2:13-14, 13:13, 13:4-8, 1:1110:13, 9:27

2 Corinthians: 5:19, 5:17, 5:5, 3:18, 12:20, 12:9-10, 6:6-7, 1:18-19, 8:9, 10:1, 5:17, 12:7

Galatians: 5:22, 5:19-23, 5:18, 6:9-10, 5:23, 2:20, 6:1

Ephesians: 1:13-14, 1:13-14, 2:1-3, 5:2, 1:20, 4:22-24, 4:2-3, 2:7-8, 4:32, 5:5-9, 3:16-17, 2:8, 4:2, 3:16, 5:17-25, 1:17

Philippians: 4:8, 2:7-8, 2:13, 4:4, 1:2, 3:9, 5:11, 2:5-8, 3:10

Colossians: 1:15-16, 3:12-17, 4:7, 1:7, 1:16, 15:1,8,16, 3:13, 3:12-15

1 Thessalonians: 1:6, 4:16-17, 3:16, 1:11, 2:23-26

2 Thessalonians: 1:6, 2:7-8, 1:6

2 Timothy: 3:10, 2:24, 2:25

Titus: 3:5, 3:2-3

Hebrews: 12:3, 12:2, 12:1-2, 11:6, 1:1-2, 12:2, 10:36, 11:6

James: 3:18, 1:3-4, 1:21, 1:5, 3:171

1 Peter: 5:7, 4:12-13, 2:3, 3:4, 3:18, 3:18-20, 3:15, 3:14 5:5-6

2 Peter: 3:9, 1:3, 1:5-11, 1:5-7, 3:9

1 John: 4:9, 4:4, 3:1, 4:7-12, 4:16, 2:3-6

Revelation: 21:3

# Benediction

" The grace of our Lord Jesus Christ, the love of God, and the communion of the Holy Ghost, be with you all." Amen, amen, amen. 2 Cor. 13:14.

MAY GOD BE GLORIFIED FOR THE GREAT THINGS HE HAS DONE IN OUR WORLD.

Books previously published by the author Grace Dola Balogun by Grace Religious Books Publishing & Distributors, Inc.

**PRAYER THE SOURCE OF STRENGTH FOR LIFE – English Edition**

*Prayer the Source of Strength for Life* is a powerful book that will energize your spirit to pray more and more until the prayer is part of your life and until the gate of heaven is opened and your prayer is answered. Your prayer life will change your life.

**LA ORACION FUENTE DE FORTALEZA PARA LA VIDA – Spanish Edition.**

Dios nos dio el poder de la oracion, quiere que lo usemos; debemos illamar, comunicarnos con el en todo lo que estemos pasando. El espera saber de nosotros.

*Spirit Power Volume I and II* both discuss the power of the Holy Spirit in the life of believers

The Power of the Spirit of God begins from the creation of the world up until today. That power will also continue until Christ returns to reign. Hallelujah!

## THE CROSS AND THE CRUCIFIXION

Our Lord Jesus Christ died on the Cross to bring forth love and compassion. Sin's impact on human life brings all other evil into our world, from one society to another society, from one culture to another.

But in Christ, we are clothed with His holiness. We have the gift of eternal life. The gate of heaven is open and we are eligible for our inheritance in heaven.

Hallelujah! Hosanna in the Highest. Jesus Christ paid it all, unto Him all we owe. The Cross of Christ is the Cross of joy, peace, and righteousness to all who believe in Him.

# About the Author

Grace Dola Balogun graduated from Fordham University Graduate School of Religion and Religious Education in the year 2010 with an M.A. in Religion and Religious Education. She has been a prayer mentor and advisor for many Christians of all denominations since 1988.

Visit her online at:
gracereligiousbookspublishers.com
Prayerstrengthforlife.com
Spiritpower.info
salvationcompleted.com
Facebook
GSTwitter@prayersource

# To Order This Book

To order additional copies of this book,
please E-mail:
info@gracereligiousbookspublishers.com

This book may also be ordered from 30,000
wholesalers, retailers, and booksellers in
the U. S., and in Canada and over
100 countries globally.

To contact Grace Dola Balogun for an
interview or a speaking engagement,
please E-mail:
info@gracereligiousbookspublishers.com

The Spirit and the bride say, "Come!"
And let the one who hears say, "Come!"
Let the one who is thirsty come;
and let the one who wishes take
the free gift of the water of life.

Revelation 22:17

*MARANATHA!*

*COME, LORD JESUS!*

www.ingramcontent.com/pod-product-compliance
Lightning Source LLC
Chambersburg PA
CBHW051452290426
44109CB00016B/1724